W9-AOD-146

Usborne

Unicorns Puzzle Pad

Illustrated by Jenny Winstanley, Helen Graper, Helen Prole, The Boy Fitz Hammond, Jordan Wray, Tim Budgen, Sarah Ward and Lucy Semple

Designed by Sharon Cooper

Written by Kate Nolan

Find and circle...
1
...6 fireflies...
...7 flags...
...and 5 elves.

Can you fit the unicorns' names into the grid?

Each unicorn only collects flowers with a number that can be divided by the number on its bag. Circle the unicorn who will collect the most flowers.

Spot 4 differences between the pictures below.

Add up the numbers to find out how long Zephyra took to complete the course, and write the total in the final flag.

Can you fill in the missing vowels to complete these unicorn words?

Can you find a nine-letter word? Move from one letter to the next along the dotted lines, using each letter only once.

Circle the 3 pieces that complete the picture.

Are there more unicorns with a pink horn or pink hooves?

Can you find all the tree names in the grid?

S	N	O	H	A	Z	E	L	E	R
T	S	U	F	C	H	O	A	K	C
E	H	Y	G	L	S	W	O	L	H
Y	A	U	C	H	N	I	D	B	E
P	E	L	E	A	S	L	A	E	S
M	Y	W	L	L	M	L	H	E	T
J	L	T	D	T	Y	O	S	C	N
R	L	P	E	A	D	W	R	H	U
Y	O	A	R	Y	H	O	B	E	T
A	H	R	O	W	A	N	U	R	L

BEECH
ELDER
OAK
CHESTNUT
HAZEL
SYCAMORE
ROWAN
WILLOW
YEW
HOLLY

The more starberries the unicorns eat, the longer it takes them to get down their paths. Circle the unicorn who will eat the fewest berries and get to the end of their path first.

Spot 4 differences between the pictures below.

Can you find and circle 9 rainbow apples?

Can you complete the words by joining up pairs of clouds?

Meadow is going to meet Moonflower, but whichever way she goes, there are obstacles that add time to her journey. Draw along the quickest route.

Fill in the shapes that have orange spots to see the hidden picture.

Can you spot the picture that is different from the others?

Guide Starlight across the stepping stones to meet Sylvia.

Can you help the fairies finish the cupcakes by drawing on the decorations? The numbers on the jars tell you how many of each decoration can be used, and each cake must have the same amount.

At the bottom of the page, circle the group of stars that the unicorns have spotted in the night sky.

Fill in the grid so that all four symbols appear in every row and column.

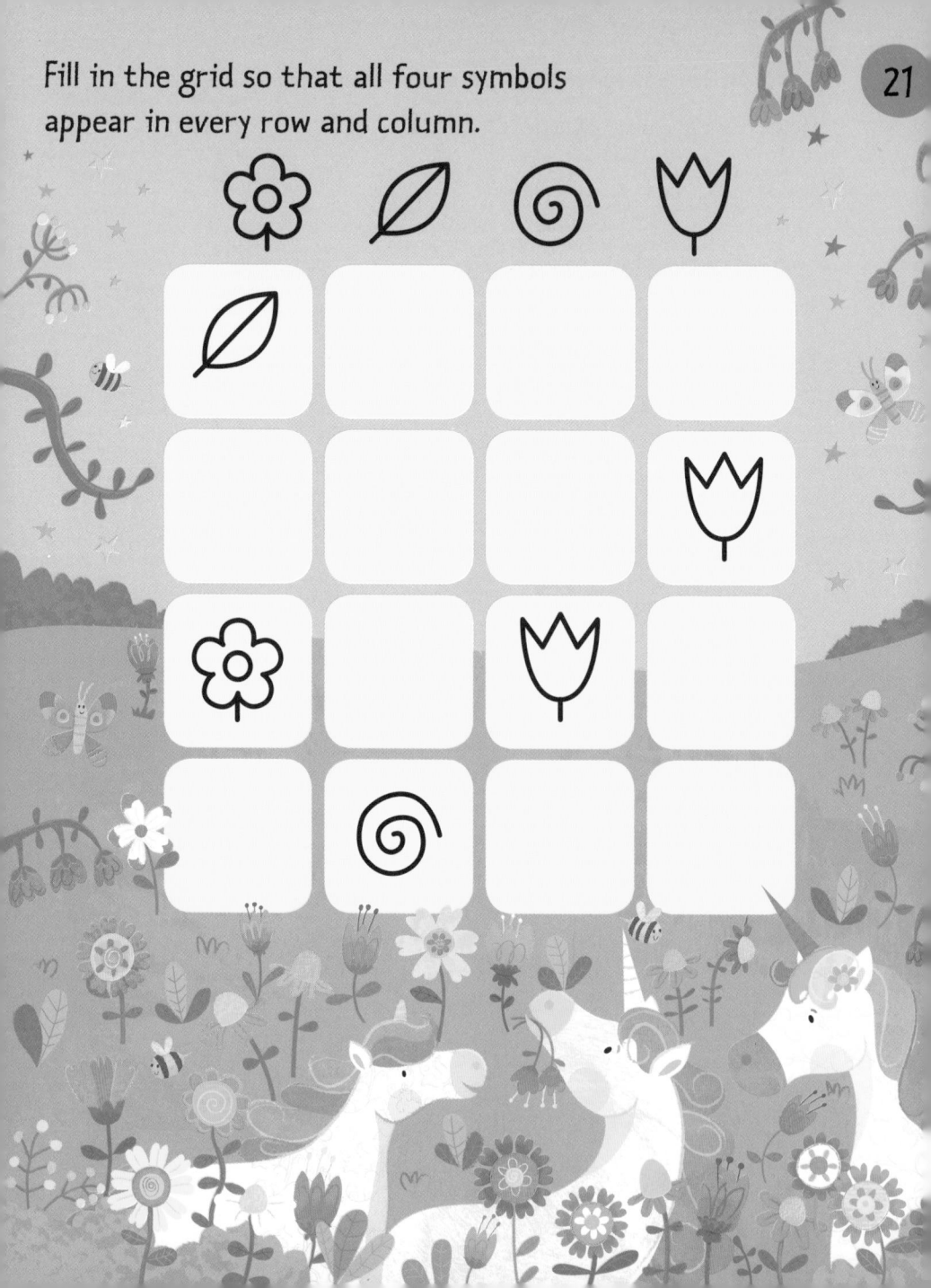

The sign on each item tells you its price in spangles.
3 different items cost 20 spangles altogether.
Which ones are they?

Can you help the unicorns find out which gemstones are in each bowl by unscrambling the letters on the labels?

Draw the other half of this unicorn picture.

Find and circle 8 lily pads...
...6 toadstools...
...4 bees...
...and 3 frogs.

Can you spot the only star in the sky with six points?

Draw a path through the toadstools for Tom and Talia. At each row, they can only pass between toadstools with odd numbers of spots.

Which silhouette matches these unicorns picking flowers?

Can you find Claribelle's crown?

Claribelle

Guide the unicorns through the spooky forest to the castle, avoiding goblins along the way.

Find the number patterns on these strings of bunting, then add the missing numbers to the empty flags.

Look at the things on the shelves for one minute, then turn over and circle the ones you remember.

Look at the other side of this page to find out how to do this puzzle.

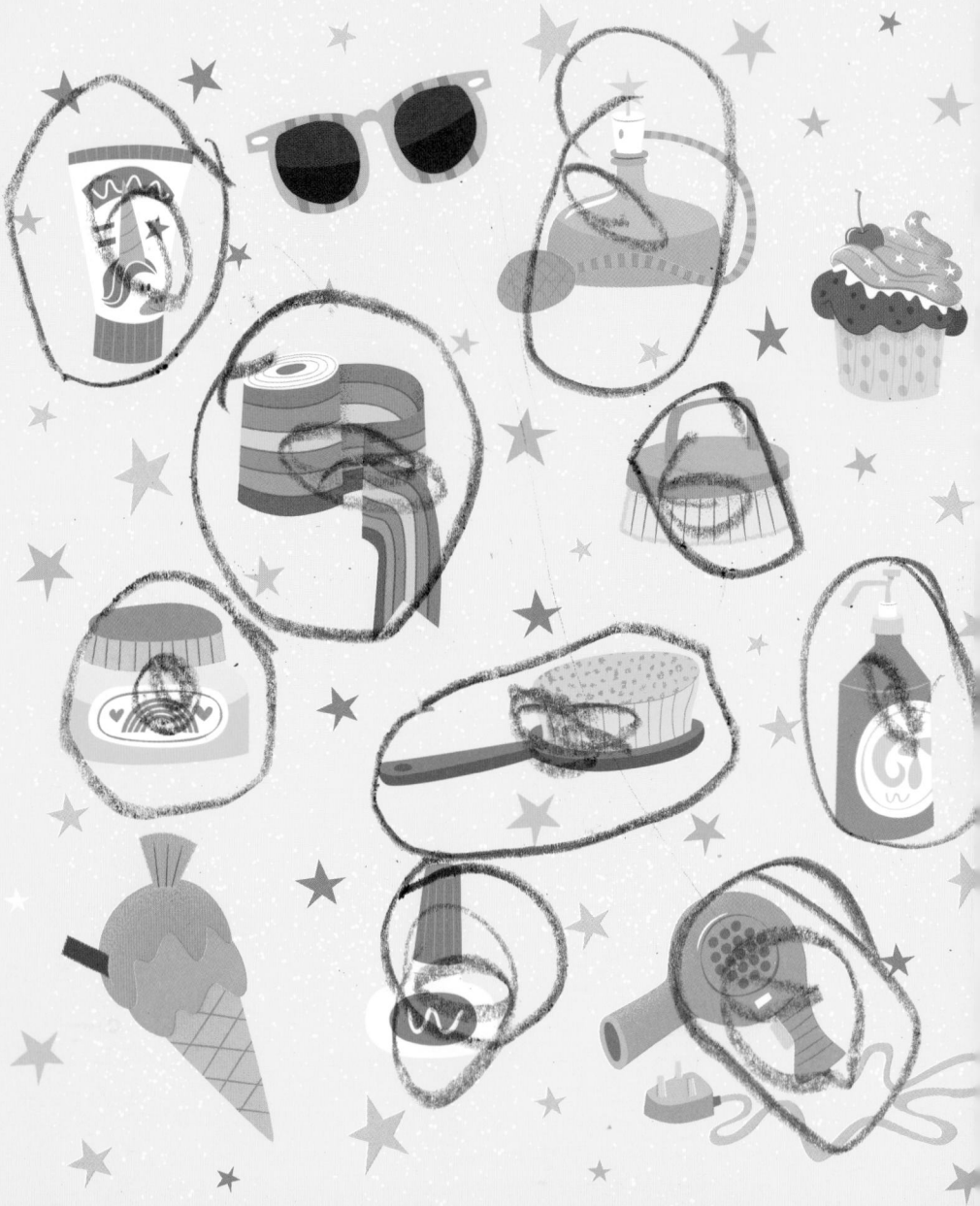

Circle Yola's unicorn. She has a purple horn and a bow, but no flowers in her mane.

Connect the even-numbered dots in number order to see who's in the meadow with Molly.

Find the path that will lead Azura to the castle in the clouds.

Can you spot 13 mistakes in this unicorn story?

Once upon a tim, there was a unicorn calld Thora, who lived in a magical castel high up in the clowds. Life in the castle with the uther unicorns wos very peaseful. Evry day, they

played together. At night, thay would watch shooting stars befor bedtime. But Thora longed to sea what was beyond the castle walls, so won day, she soared away, seeking advencher...

It's bedtime, so Zarina is rounding up the unicorn foals. It takes 5 seconds to fetch each one that is standing up, and 15 seconds for each one that's lying down. How long will it take to round up all the foals outside the stable?

Find these two groups in the picture below.

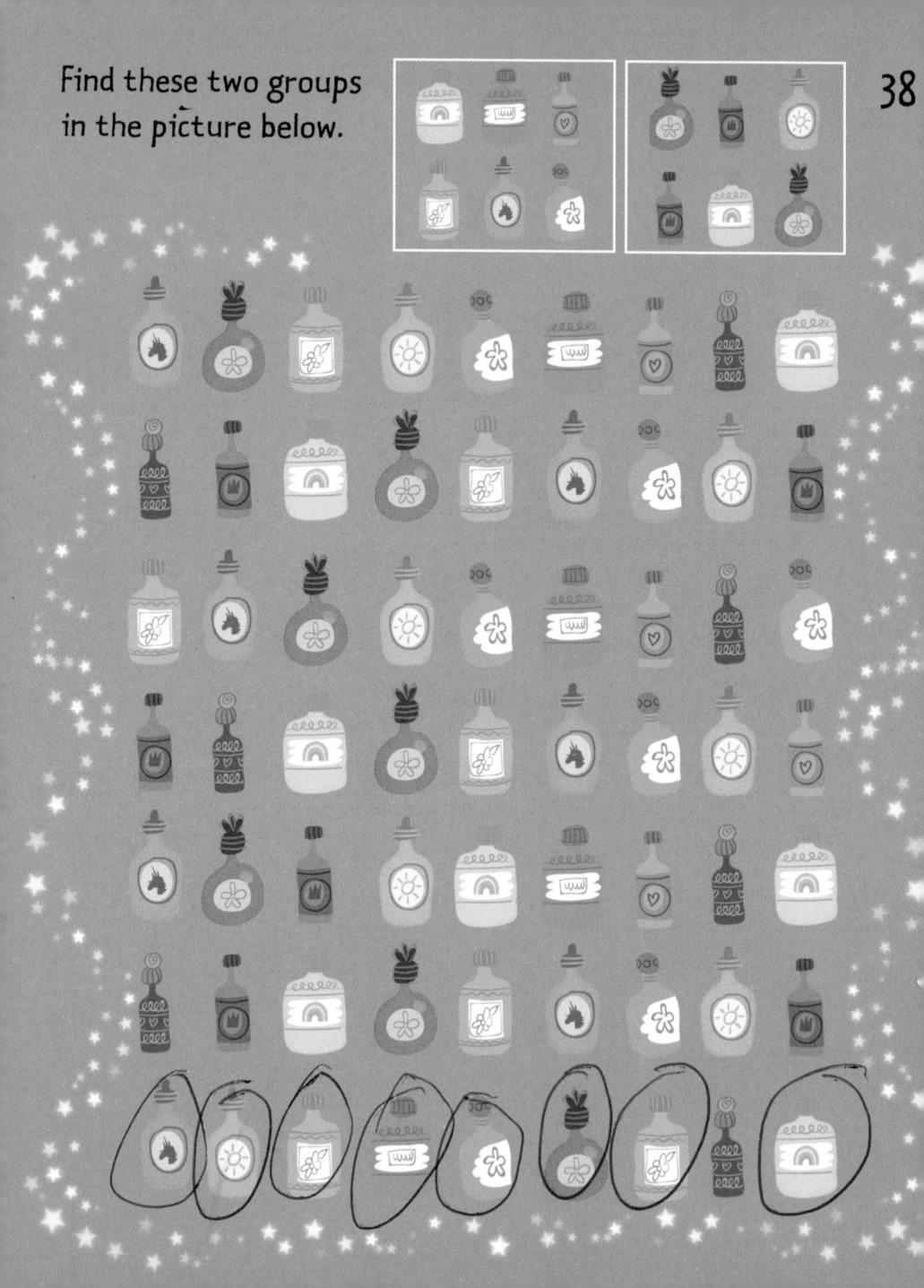

Can you fit these weather words into the grid?

Can you help Hettie find her way back to her friends?

In this grid, the numbers in every 3-square row, column and diagonal must add up to 15. Write the missing numbers in the empty squares.

Spot 4 differences between the pictures below.

It's bedtime, but 7 of the unicorn foals are hiding. Can you find and circle each one?

Use the clues to find out which unicorn is which, then write the correct name on each sign.

1. Juniper has a striped tail.
2. Marilla has orange hooves.
3. Sparkles is standing up.
4. Caspian has a blue mane.

Circle the 3 pieces that complete the picture.

Add spots to the empty toadstools so the spots along each side of the triangle add up to 20. Each one must have between 1 and 9 spots, and none of them should have the same amount.

Are there enough magic gems in the caves for each unicorn to collect four?

If 6 unicorns can eat 4 sacks of Sparkle Snacks, and 10 foals can eat 2 sacks, how many sacks can 3 unicorns and 5 foals eat?

.....

Can you write the unicorns' names on the signs?

- Cloud is next to Lena, who has flowers in her mane.
- The rainbow apples are in front of Arrow's stall.
- Bonnie is between Chip (the smallest unicorn) and Skye.

Which of the unicorn foals at the bottom of the page comes next in the sequence?

Circle the photo that has just been taken.

The fairy princess can take two passengers in her carriage. How many trips will she need to make so that all the fairies in the park can have a moonlit ride?

Fill in the blank squares so that each block, row and column contains all six letters of the word FOREST.

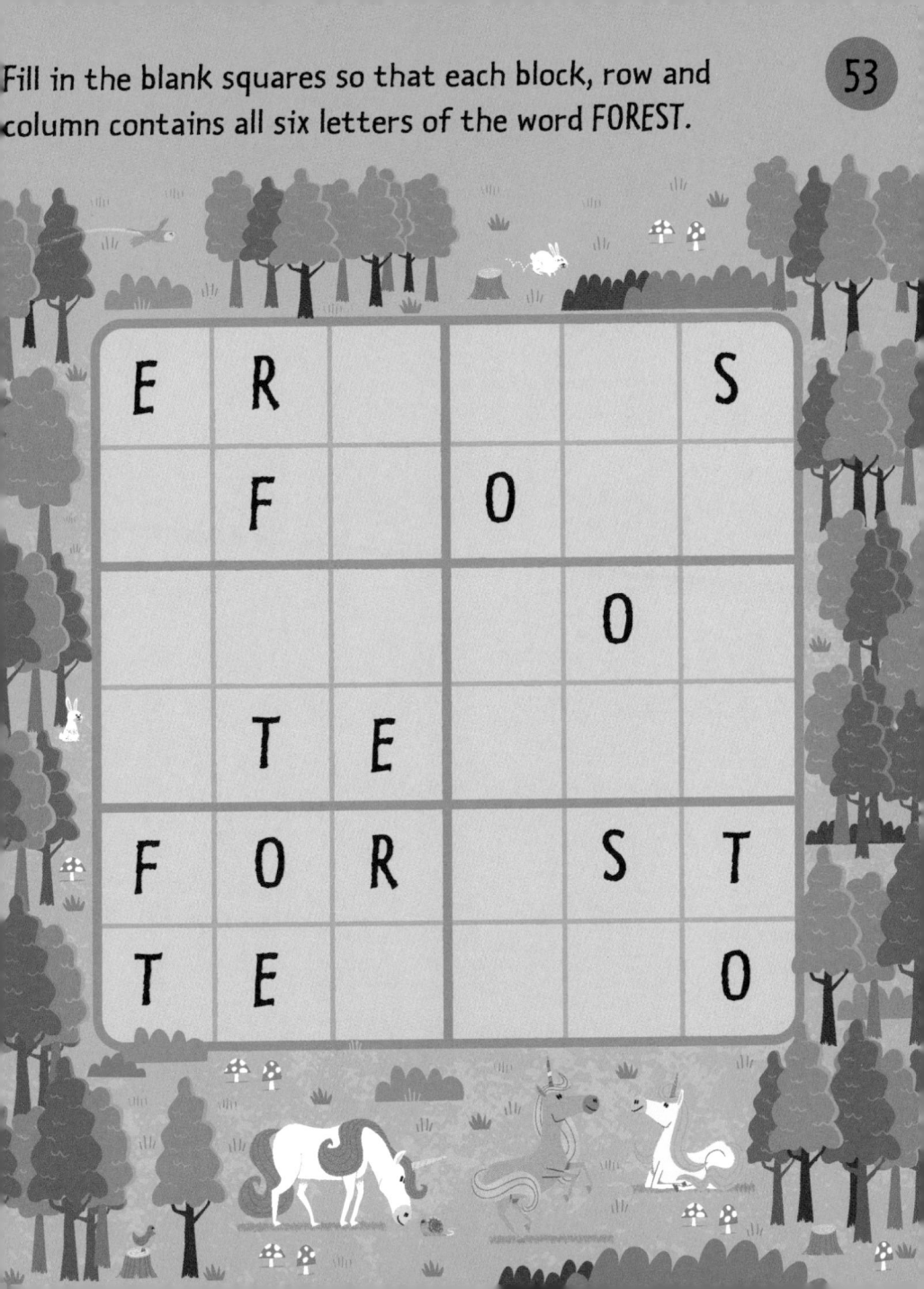

E	R				S
	F		O		
				O	
	T	E			
F	O	R		S	T
T	E				O

Can you find all of these unicorn treats in the grid?

S	C	A	C	O	R	N	S	P	F
B	T	A	F	N	U	T	S	E	A
S	H	A	N	L	S	A	P	A	I
L	A	P	B	D	N	C	C	C	R
A	E	P	F	E	Y	H	A	H	Y
T	L	L	S	N	R	C	K	E	C
E	O	E	R	T	Y	R	A	S	A
P	R	S	Z	A	D	W	I	N	K
S	P	R	O	U	T	S	I	E	E
A	C	A	R	R	O	T	S	R	S

APPLES BERRIES PETALS

FAIRY CAKE ACORNS

CARROTS CANDY CANE SPROUTS

PEACHES NUTS

Find and circle 5 rainbow apples, 3 owls and a magic wand.

Follow the trails to the stalls to find out each unicorn's name.

Can you spot the only unicorn without a twin?

How many bottles of potion can be made from the ingredients on the table? Write your answer on the scroll.

Read the descriptions below, then draw a line to match each unicorn to the name that you think suits it best.

Crystal lives in a sparkling ice castle.

Starshine loves to gallop when the moon is full.

Posy frolics in flowery meadows in spring.

Storm can control the weather with her horn.

Spot 4 differences between the pictures below.

The winner of this party game has striped tights and pink shoes, but no hat. Who is it?

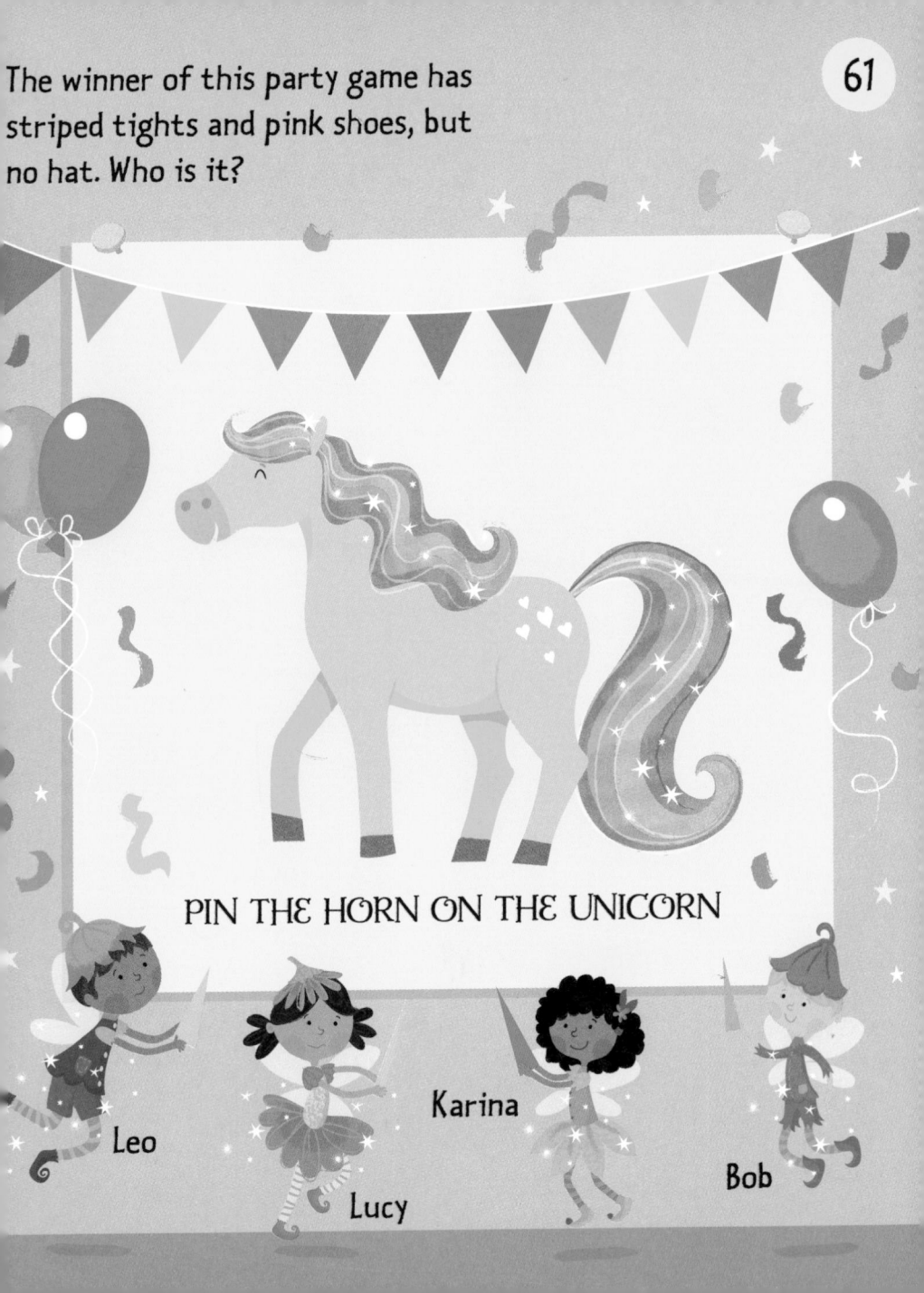

Can you find the fairy tale characters in the grid?

S	K	O	H	Y	Z	A	L	E	J
L	G	R	E	T	E	L	N	K	A
G	A	O	D	R	F	W	O	F	C
R	B	E	A	N	S	T	A	L	K
A	D	L	E	T	P	R	F	H	I
N	L	W	S	H	S	O	L	A	E
D	O	J	C	W	Z	L	S	N	I
M	R	T	D	U	O	L	K	S	L
A	I	P	M	A	I	L	U	E	T
W	T	N	A	I	G	N	F	L	R

GRETEL HANSEL TROLL GIANT
WITCH GOATS BEANSTALK
JACK WOLF
GRANDMA

Draw the way through this sky racecourse, moving from square to square in the sequence shown at the bottom. You can't move diagonally, or go through any box twice.

Help Ava and Adam find Carrie's cabin.
Its door number can be divided by 2, 3, 6 and 9.

For every rainbow apple that Dancer picks, Rosehip picks two. How many apples will each unicorn pick from the trees?

Dancer: ..... Rosehip: .....

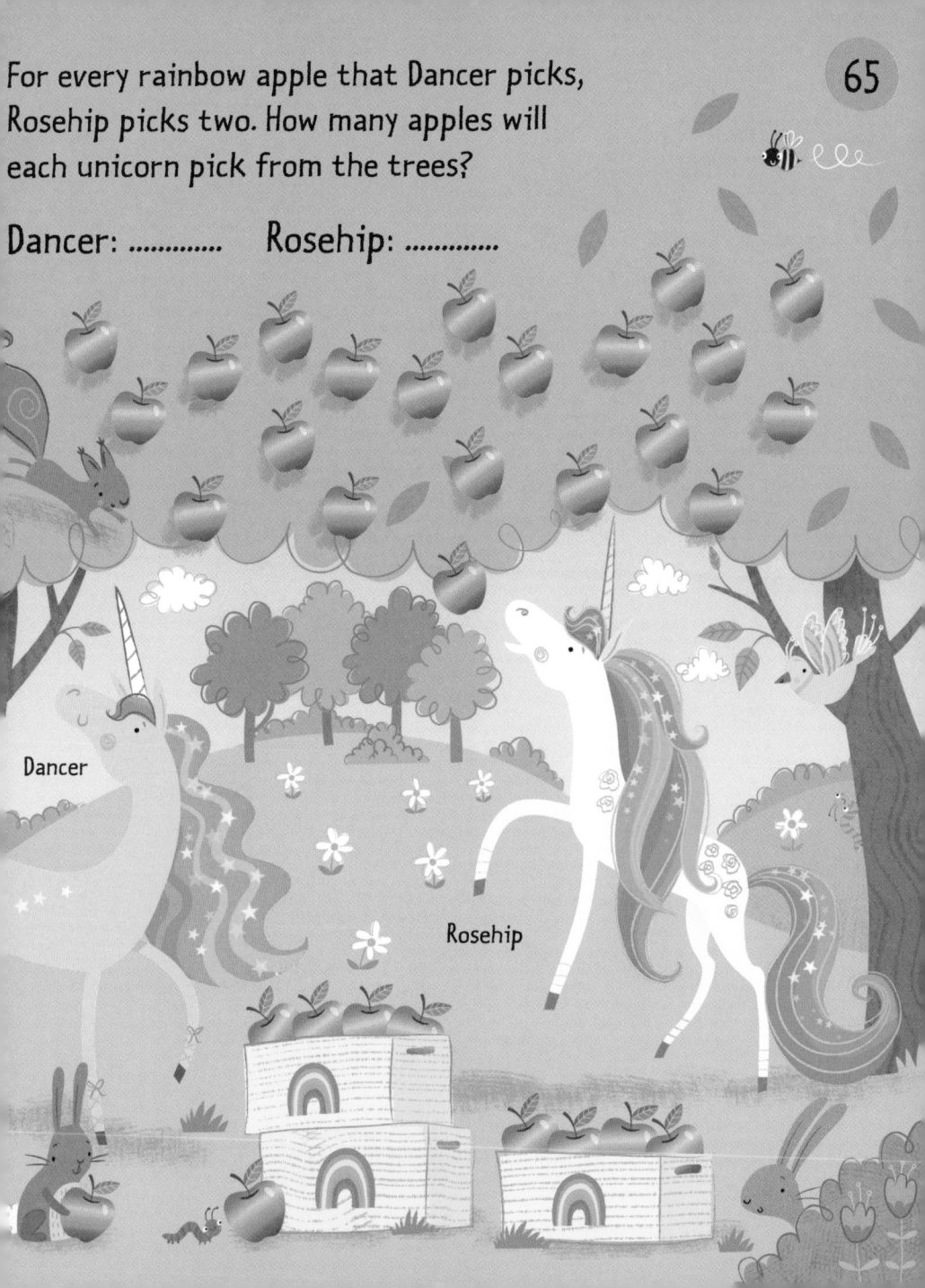

Help Fernando the fairy finish his magic painting by shading every shape that has a blue spot.

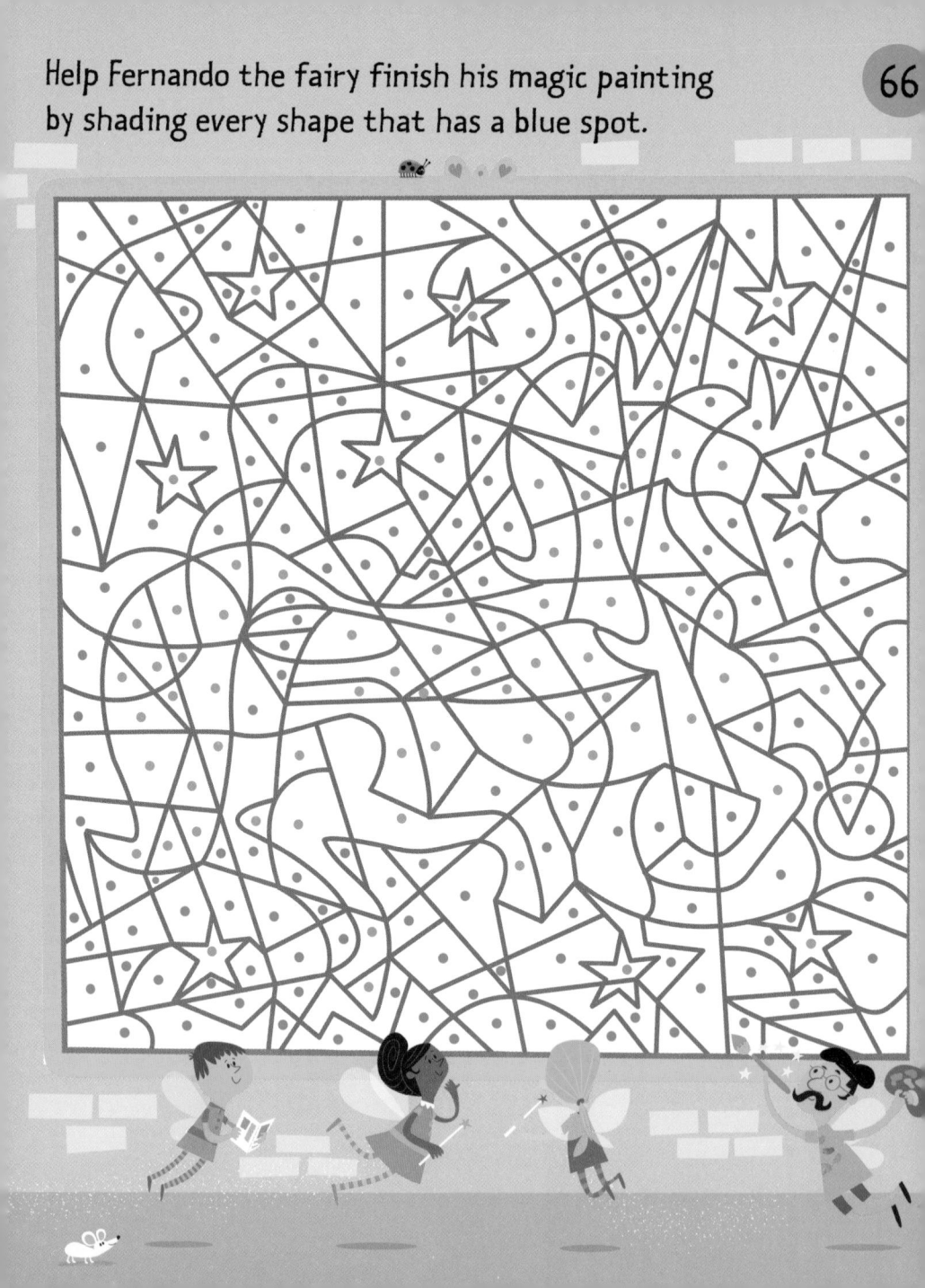

Complete these magical jokes by matching the questions with their punchlines.

How many 'bouquets of the day' can Petal and Blossom make from the flowers in the field?

Find a route for Lilabelle to look at every butterfly and finish where she started, without crossing her own path.

Fill in the grid so that all four symbols appear in every row and column.

Find all the unicorns' names in the grid.

R	N	O	T	S	I	L	V	E	R
S	S	U	F	C	H	A	I	C	A
E	H	H	G	L	N	A	O	L	M
V	A	U	I	W	A	W	D	H	Y
O	D	L	X	R	S	S	A	O	E
M	O	O	N	L	I	G	H	T	W
J	W	Y	I	I	O	N	S	A	O
A	S	P	U	A	M	I	U	P	P
Y	I	P	N	Y	H	O	B	T	A
A	M	E	T	H	Y	S	T	H	L

Fill in the grid so that all four symbols appear in every row and column.

Circle the cupcake that is different from all the others at the fairy bakery.

The numbers in this square go up in a pattern. Can you find the pattern and fill in the empty boxes?

	8		16		24
28			40		48
	56			68	
76					96
	104		112		120
124		132		140	

Can you draw 6 stars in the grid without putting 3 in a row in any direction?

Match up the words with opposite meanings.
Which toadstool isn't one of a pair?

Circle the 4 pieces that complete the picture.

Add up the numbers to find out how many seconds each unicorn takes in the rainbow race. Who will be the first to reach the wishing well?

Spot 5 differences between the pictures below.

Which unicorn will reach the wishing well?

Are there enough shooting stars for each fairy to catch three?

Match up the fairies to their unicorns.
Which fairy won't be riding today?

Solve the calculations to find out how strong the unicorns' magic powers are, then add them up and circle the most powerful unicorn.

Healing: 17 + 13 =
Speed: 9 x 5 =
Invisibility: 40 ÷ 10 =
Total power:

Healing: 50 - 30 =
Speed: 80 ÷ 2 =
Invisibility: 13 + 5 =
Total power:

Healing: 6 x 10 =
Speed: 27 - 15 =
Invisibility: 10 ÷ 2 =
Total power:

Healing: 16 + 9 =
Speed: 12 x 2 =
Invisibility: 40 - 9 =
Total power:

Circle the photo that has just been taken.

Fill in the blank clouds, so that each number is the sum of the two directly beneath it.

Which path should Petal take to put the star on top of the Christmas tree?

Connect the odd-numbered dots in number order to see who's exploring the coral reef.

Draw stars on 4 of the unicorns' blankets, hearts on half of the remaining ones, and stripes on half of the rest. How many are left with plain blankets?

Can you spot the unicorn that is different from all the rest at the toy shop?

Can you find 8 gemstones in the letter chain?

Circle the unicorn foal who isn't joined to a fairy.

Can you find out where each basket of rainbow apples should be delivered? Do the calculations, then draw a line between each tag and its matching stable.

Can you find these mythical creatures in the grid?

S	R	O	H	Y	Z	A	L	E	R
G	A	D	R	A	G	O	N	K	P
R	O	I	D	R	S	W	O	L	I
I	A	C	P	H	O	E	N	I	X
F	D	L	E	E	S	L	L	E	I
F	L	W	S	N	T	L	A	F	E
I	O	J	B	P	T	I	T	C	I
N	E	M	O	N	G	A	R	L	X
M	E	R	M	A	I	D	U	P	S
L	H	R	O	F	T	N	S	R	S

ELF
PIXIE
MERMAID
CENTAUR
DRAGON
PHOENIX
GRIFFIN
FAIRY
GNOME
SPRITE

Circle the unicorn that matches the silhouette.

Use the clues to find out what each unicorn will get from the Snack Shack, and draw a line to match them up.

Circle the 3 pieces that complete the picture.

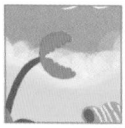

ivide the field into seven areas by drawing fences. Each rea must contain the same number of squares as rainbow arrots. The first carrot has been fenced in already.

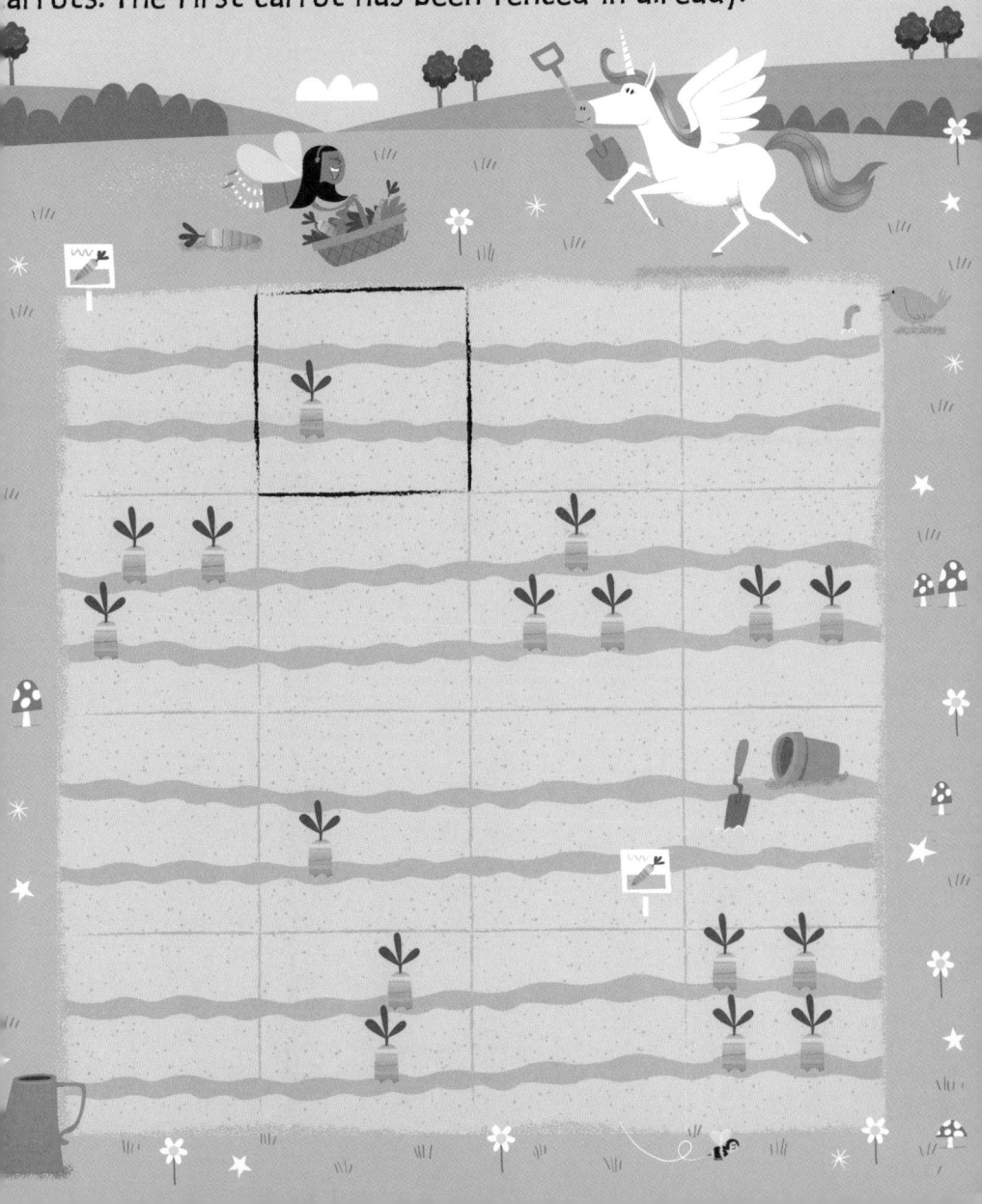

Follow the sparkly trails to find out who set off each magic firework.

Circle 4 pink flags, 2 balloons, a butterfly and a dog.

Can you circle these 5 parts of the picture?

Use the symbols below to help you finish this joke:
How do bees brush their hair?

Each unicorn needs two apples and three carrots.
How many of each are needed altogether?

Apples: ..... Carrots: .....

Can you circle these 5 parts of the picture?

Help Tilly find her way through the toadstools to reach the fairies in the middle.

Draw the other half of this castle. Use the grid to help you.

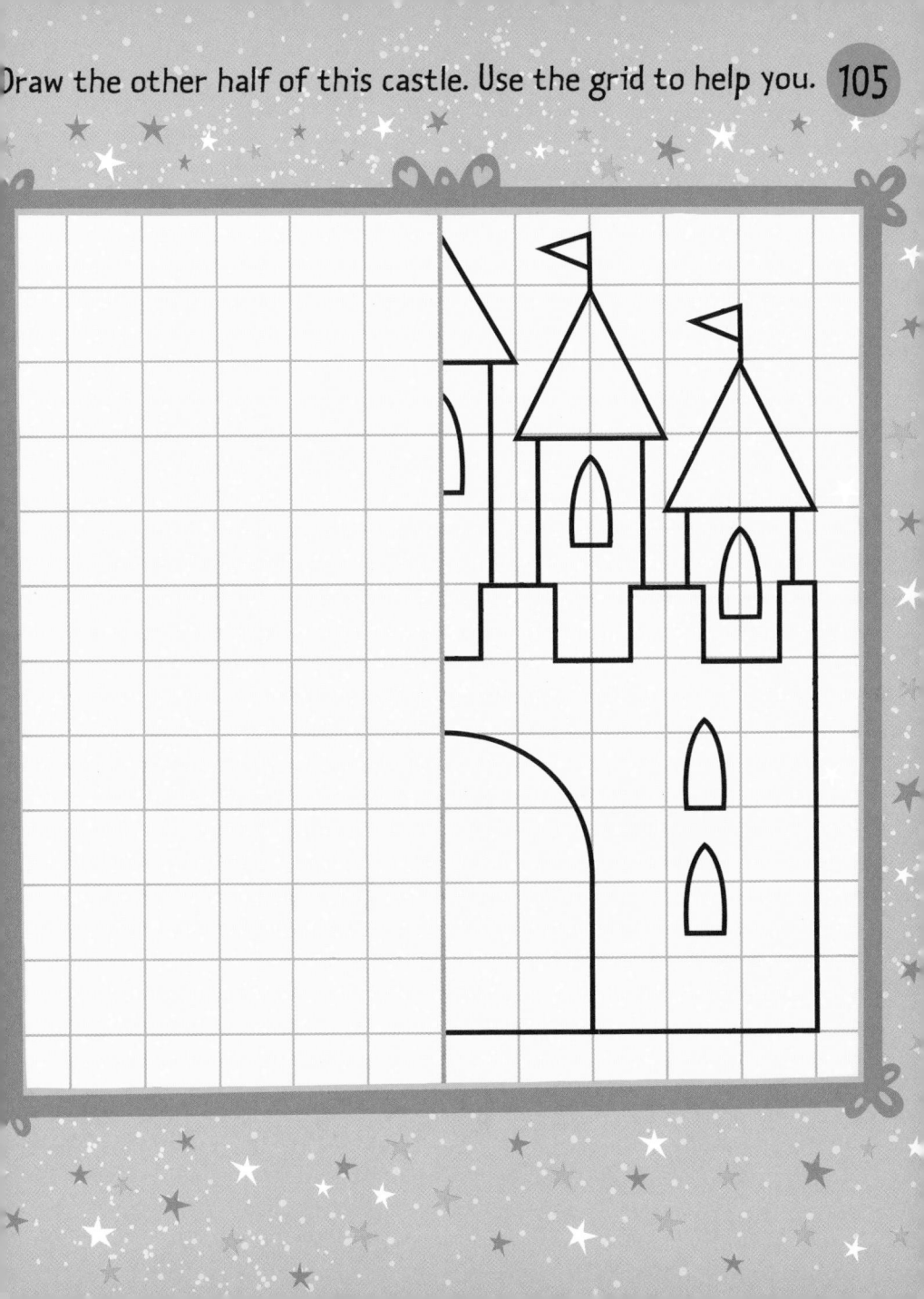

Are there more sea unicorns or unicorn seahorses?

Spot 5 differences between the pictures below.

The fastest time ever galloped on the rainbow racetrack is 1 minute and 29 seconds. Add up Flossy's times on the flags. Has she beaten the record? Circle yes or no.

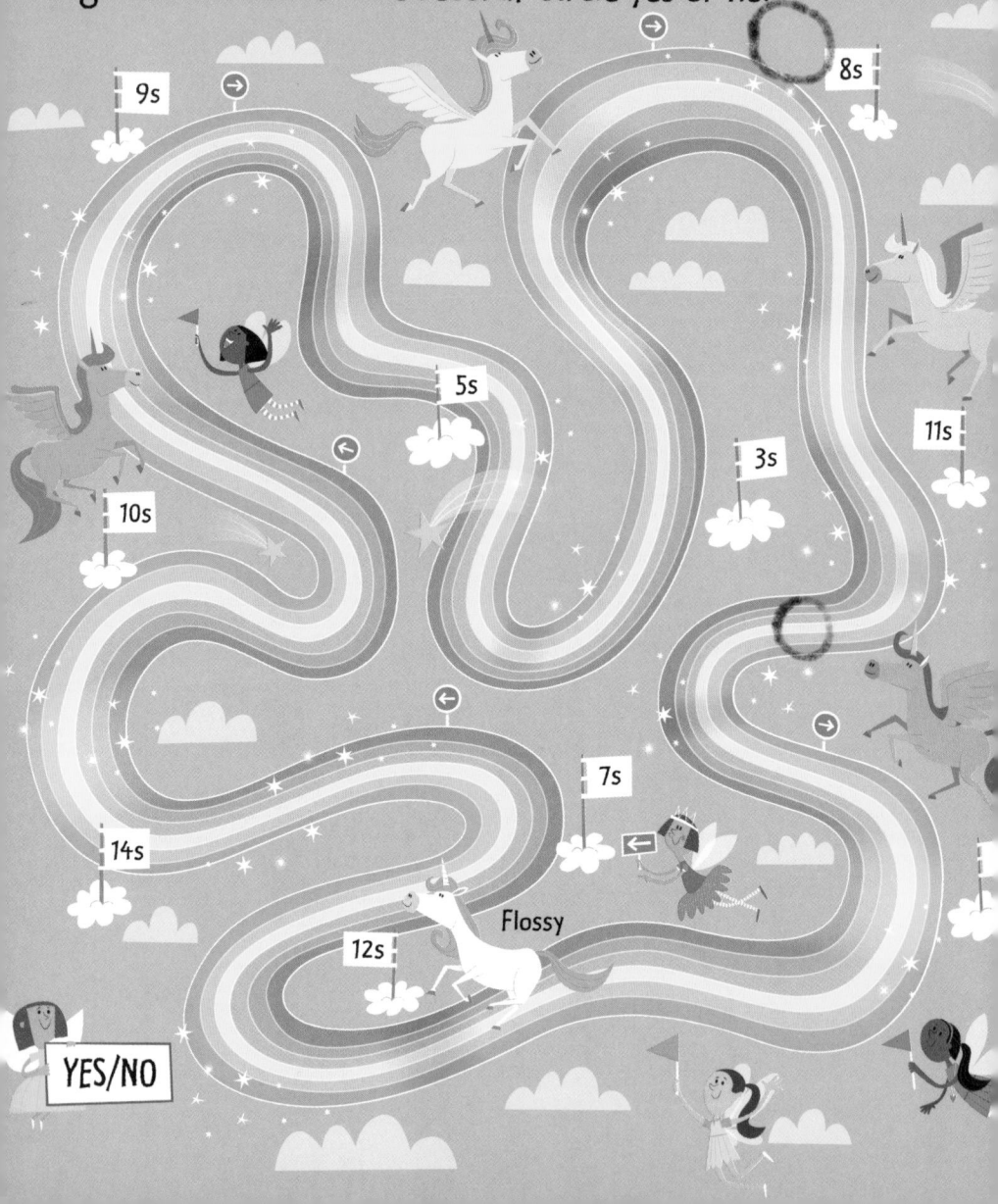

f all the unicorns follow these instructions, which one will reach the wishing well?

square forward, 1 square north, 2 squares west, 3 squares south, 1 square east, 1 square south, 2 squares east, 2 squares north

The grid below is made up of 9 blocks, each with 9 squares. Fill in the blank squares so that every block, row and column contains all the digits 1 to 9.

6		9	1			5	4	7
	4	1		6			8	
5	2		7		4		9	6
1			8		3		6	9
8	9	4	6	5		3	2	1
		6	4	1		7	5	8
3		8	2	4				
			5		6	8	3	4
4		5	3	9	8	6	1	

Which silhouette matches this row of unicorns?

Who will reach the basket of delicious rainbow apples?

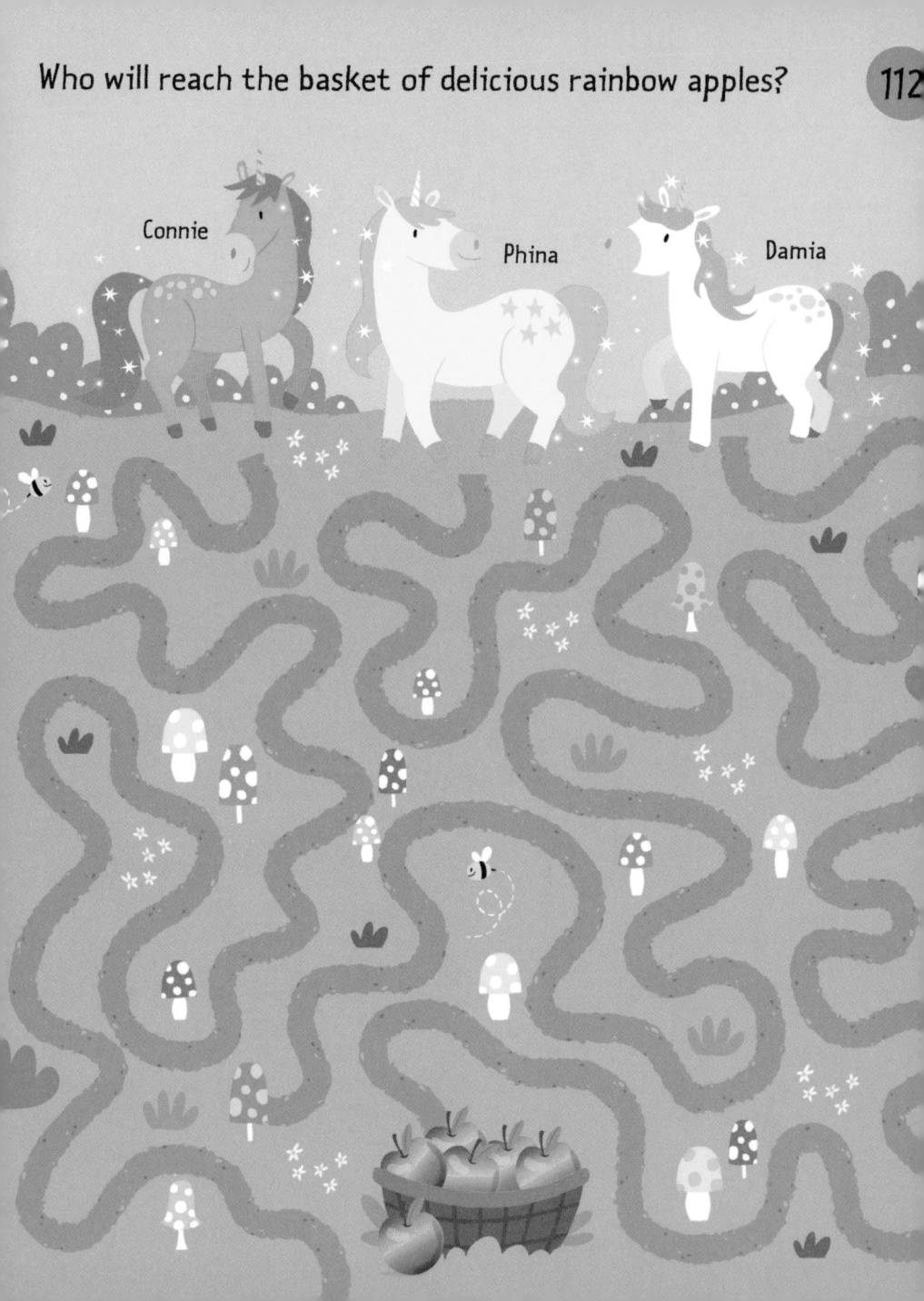

Help Celesta find her way through the snowy mountains to the castle, avoiding any cracks in the ice.

Write a word on each leaf that can be made by changing just one letter of the word before it. There is a clue on each leaf to help you.

Cross out every letter that is one of a pair. What word can you spell with the five letters that are left?

Spot 4 differences between the pictures below.

ind out who scored the most points at the Unicorn Games
y filling in the missing numbers, then write 1st, 2nd, 3rd
r 4th on the dotted lines below each column.

THE UNICORN GAMES
• RESULTS •

	Violet	Irina	Rainbow	Frank	Total
Cloud jumping	3	5	4	2	
Spell casting	5	3		6	20
Raindrop race		4		5	
Total score	16		19		
	.....	.....	.....	.....	

Circle 16 snowballs, 9 toadstools and 2 rainbow carrots.

n the unicorn show, Berry finished ahead of Floriana
ut behind Pippin. Yasmin finished behind Pippin but
head of Berry. Write 1st, 2nd, 3rd or 4th
n each unicorn's rosette.

Can you unscramble these rainbow words?

The unicorns have been picking starberries.

- Hazel picked 3 times as many as Daisy.
- Moonbeam collected 18 berries (8 more than Alfie).
- Daisy picked half as many as Alfie.

Next to their names, write how many berries each one picked.

Luna is lost in the spooky forest, and she needs your help to escape. Use the key to find out what to do at each obstacle.

Find these two groups in the picture below.

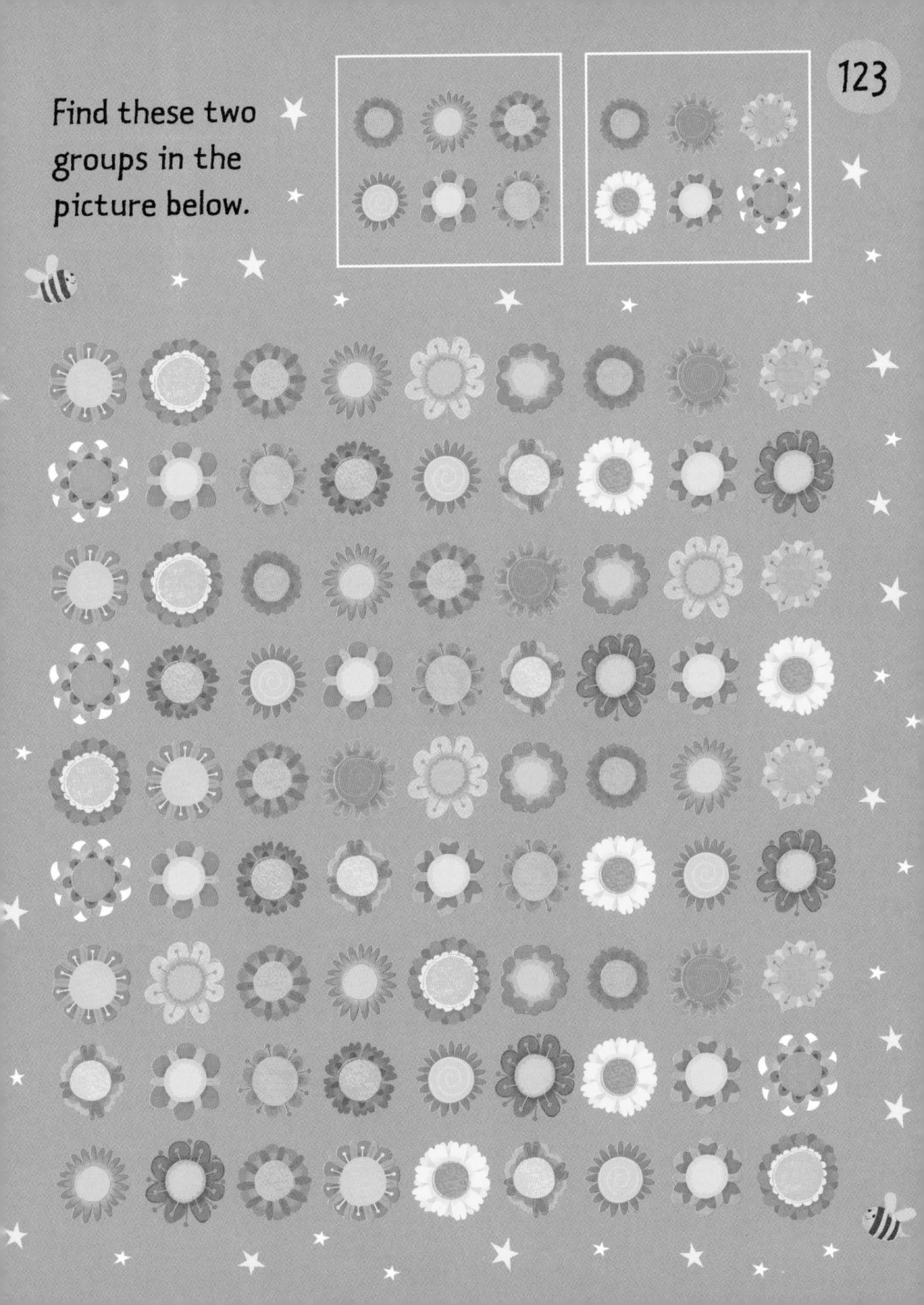

Help Firefly find her way through the clouds to the rainbow.

ach of these unicorns needs a set of magic unicorn
hoes. How many shoes will Felix the fairy have to make?

Can you fit the words below into the grid?

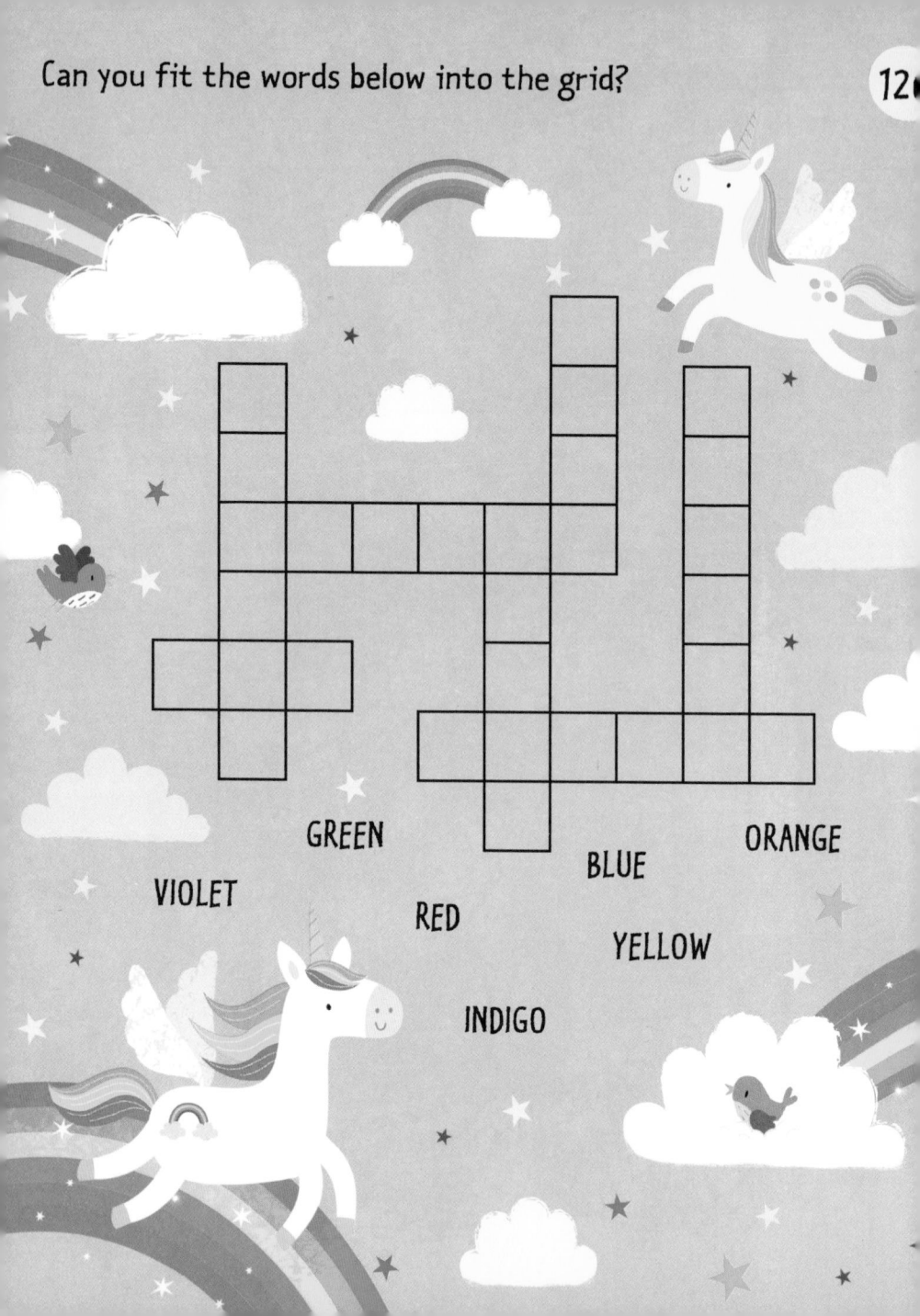

GREEN

ORANGE

BLUE

VIOLET

RED

YELLOW

INDIGO

This grid is made up of 6 blocks, each with 6 squares. Fill in the blank squares so that each block, row and column contains all the digits 1 to 6.

	1			3	2
			5		1
		3		4	
	5	6		2	
5					
2	6				

In the unicorn race, Dazzle finished before Sienna, but after Sunbeam. Thunder wasn't first, but was two places in front of Leila. No unicorn beginning with 'S' came last. Write the unicorns' names on the scoreboard below.

SCOREBOARD

1st.....

2nd..... 3rd.....

4th..... 5th.....

ind these two groups in the picture below.

Fill in the grid so all the letters in the word HORN appear in every row and column.

Are there enough rainbow carrots for each unicorn to have one?

Find and circle the unicorn picture that is different from all the others.

pot 4 differences between the pictures below.

Solve the clues to fill in the blank spaces below.

ACROSS

2. Enchantment (5)
5. A witch may ride this (10)
8. A four-leaf___ may be lucky (6)
9. Male magician or sorcerer (6)
10. Little bearded man often seen in gardens (5)
11. Magic stick (4)
12. If something is ___ it cannot be seen (9)

DOWN

1. Witch's purring pet (5, 3)
3. Magic liquid (6)
4. It's worn on a horse's foot, and some think it's lucky (9)
6. 3 downs can be made in this big, black pot (8)
7. A unicorn has just one (4)
9. Dragons, fairies and phoenixes all have these (5)

ill in the shapes that have pink
ots to see the hidden picture.

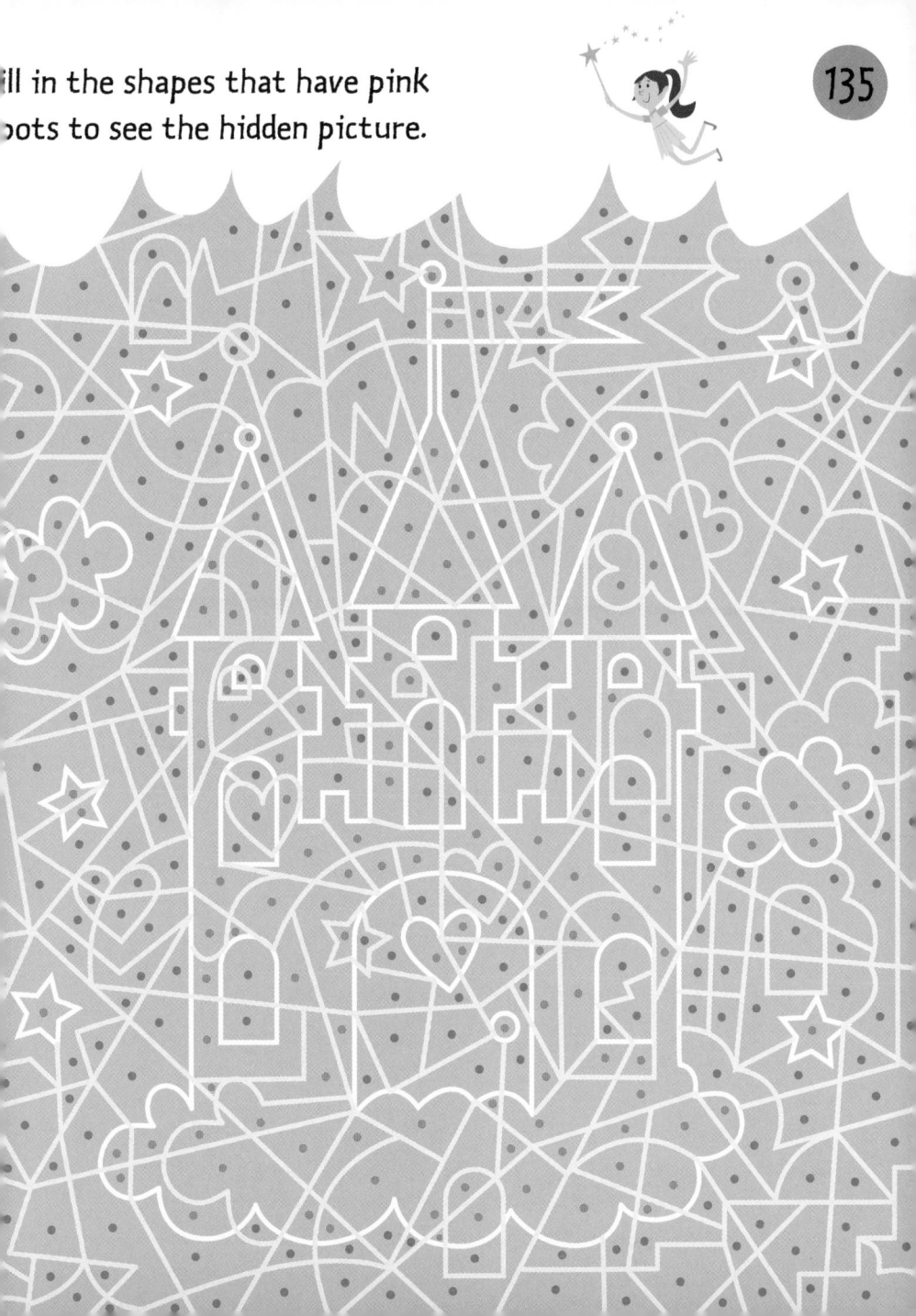

Can you circle these 5 parts of the picture?

ircle the words that can't be made with letters from he word FLOWERS. Each letter can be used only once.

Answers

1

2

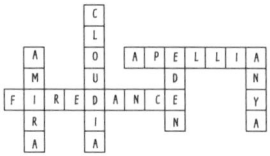

3

4

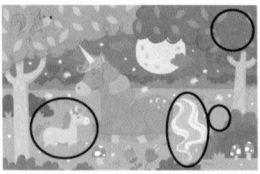

5 13.5 seconds

6 MAGIC, SPARKLE, MANE, GALLOP, LEGEND, FAIRY

7

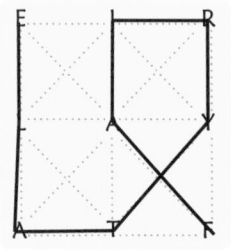

FAIRY-TALE

8

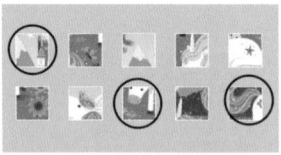

9 Pink hooves
(5 with a pink hor
6 with pink hoov

10

11

12

Answers

16

19 Each cake should have 5 sprinkles, 3 jelly beans, 1 candy cane, 2 starberries and 2 fairy flowers.

RAIN - BOW
WOOD - LAND
BUTTER - FLY
SNOW - FLAKE
DAY - DREAM
STAR - LIGHT
SUN - BEAM

17

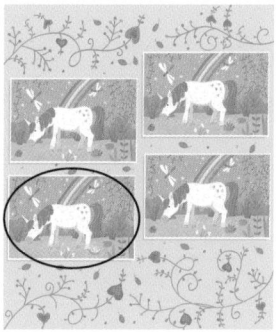

20

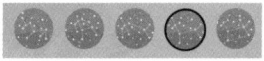

21

18

22 Hoof warmers, a rainbow apple and a cupcake

Answers

23 RUBIES, DIAMONDS, EMERALDS, PEARLS, OPALS

24

25

26

27

28 3

29

30

31 2, 4, 6, 8, 10
25, 20, 15, 10, 5
3, 6, 9, 12, 15

Answers

35

39

36 Once upon a **time**, there was a unicorn **called** Thora, who lived in a magical **castle** high up in the **clouds**. Life in the castle with the **other** unicorns **was** very **peaceful**. **Every** day, they played together. At night, **they** would watch shooting stars **before** bedtime. But Thora longed to **see** what was beyond the castle walls, so **one** day, she soared away, seeking **adventure**...

40

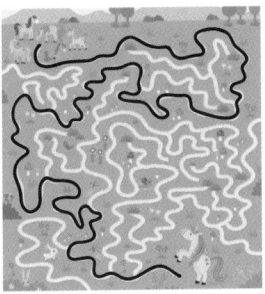

37 45 seconds

38

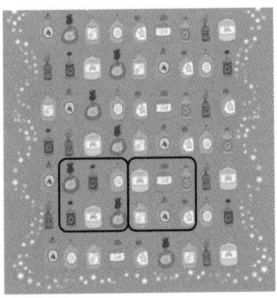

41

Answers

42

43

44

45

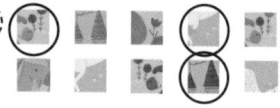

46

47

Yes. There are 16 gems for 4 unicorns.

48

3 sacks

49

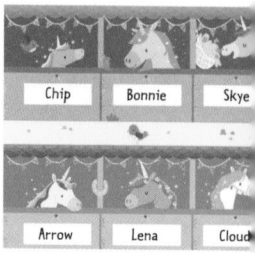

50

Answers

3 trips

E	R	O	F	T	S
S	F	T	O	E	R
R	S	F	T	O	E
O	T	E	S	R	F
F	O	R	E	S	T
T	E	S	R	F	O

54

S	C	A	C	O	R	N	S	P	F
B	T	A	F	N	U	T	S	E	A
S	H	A	N	L	S	A	P	A	I
L	A	P	B	D	N	C	C	C	R
A	E	P	F	E	Y	H	A	H	Y
T	L	L	S	N	R	C	K	E	C
E	O	E	R	T	Y	R	A	S	A
D	R	S	Z	A	D	W	I	N	K
S	P	R	O	U	T	S	I	E	E
A	C	A	R	R	O	T	S	R	S

55

56

57

58

59

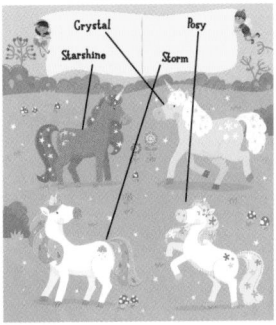

Answers

60

61

Karina

62

S	K	O	H	Y	Z	A	L	E	J
L	G	R	E	T	E	L	N	K	A
G	A	O	D	R	F	W	O	F	C
R	B	E	A	N	S	T	A	L	K
A	D	L	E	T	P	R	F	H	I
N	L	W	S	H	S	O	L	A	E
D	O	I	C	W	Z	L	S	N	I
M	R	T	D	U	O	L	K	S	L
A	I	P	M	A	I	L	U	E	T
W	T	N	A	I	G	N	F	L	R

63

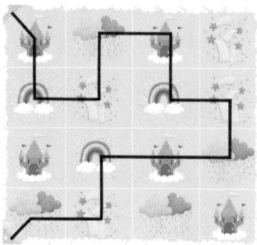

64

65

Dancer: 7

Rosehip: 14

66

67 What do you call a unicorn with no horn?
A horse
What did the sea say to the mermaid?
Nothing, it just waved.
What do fairies learn at school?
The elfabet
What do you call a wizard on a plane?
A flying sorcerer
What stories do unicorns like best?
Fairy tails

68

5 bouquets

Answers

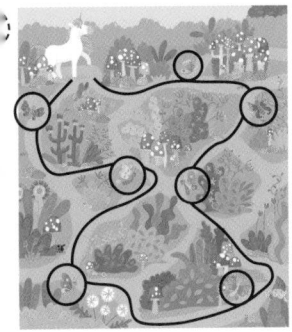

72

75

or:

73

76 SUMMER - WINTER
NORTH - SOUTH
LIGHT - DARK
DAY - NIGHT
OLD - NEW
QUIET is not one of a pair.

77

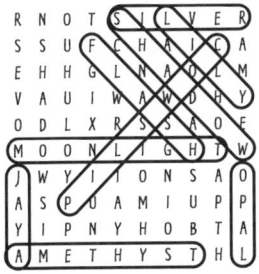

R	N	O	T	S	I	L	V	E	R		
S	S	U	F	C	H	A	I	C	A		
E	H	H	G	L	N	A	O	L	M		
V	A	U	I	W	A	W	D	H	Y		
O	D	L	X	R	S	S	A	O	E		
M	O	O	N	L	I	G	H	T	W		
J	W	Y	I	I	O	N	S	A	O		
A	S	P	U	A	M	I	U	P	P		
Y	I	P	N	Y	H	O	B	T	A		
A	M	E	T	H	Y	S	T	H	L		

74

4	8	12	16	20	24
28	32	36	40	44	48
52	56	60	64	68	72
76	80	84	88	92	96
100	104	108	112	116	120
124	128	132	136	140	144

78 Buttercup wins. (Buttercup 25: Amber 28)

Answers

79

80

Logan

81 No. There are 4 fairies and 10 shooting stars.

82

83

84

85

86

87

88 2
(4 with stars,
4 with hearts,
2 striped)

89

90 RUBY, AMBER, MOONSTONE, SAPPHIRE, OPAL, TOPAZ, DIAMOND, JADE

Answers

94

97

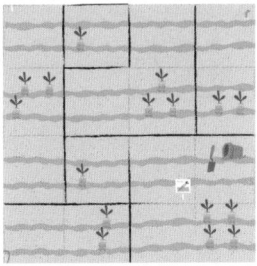

98

95

99

S	R	O	H	Y	Z	A	L	E	R	
G	A	D	R	A	G	O	N	K	P	
R	O	I	D	R	S	W	O	L	I	
I	A	C	P	H	O	E	N	I	X	
F	D	L	E	E	S	L	L	E	I	
F	L	W	S	N	T	L	A	F	E	
I	O	J	B	P	T	I	T	C	I	
N	E	M	O	N	G	A	R	L	X	
M	E	R	M	A	I	D	U	P	S	
L	H	R	O	F	T	N	S	R	S	

96

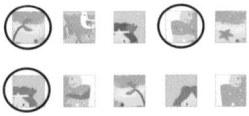

Answers

100

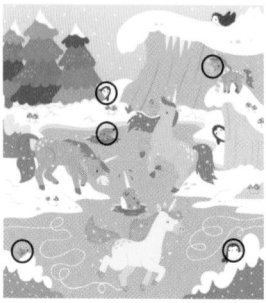

104

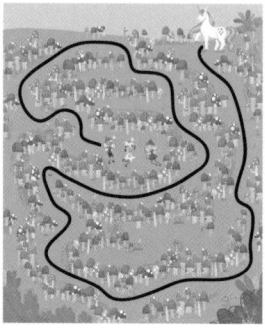

107

101 They use a honeycomb.

105

108

102 Apples: 12
Carrots: 18

103

106 More unicorn seahorses
(4 sea unicorns:
7 unicorn seahorses)

109

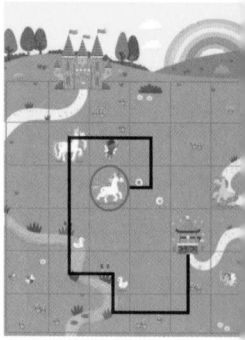

Answers

6	8	9	1	3	2	5	4	7
7	4	1	9	6	5	2	8	3
5	2	3	7	8	4	1	9	6
1	5	7	8	2	3	4	6	9
8	9	4	6	5	7	3	2	1
2	3	6	4	1	9	7	5	8
3	6	8	2	4	1	9	7	5
9	1	2	5	7	6	8	3	4
4	7	5	3	9	8	6	1	2

113

114 MOON, MOAN, MEAN, BEAN, BEAM

2

115

116

117

	Violet	Irina	Rainbow	Frank	Total
Cloud jumping	3	5	4	2	14
Spell casting	5	3	6	6	20
Raindrop race	8	4	9	5	26
Total score	16	12	19	13	60
	2nd	4th	1st	3rd	

118

119

1st: Pippin
2nd: Yasmin
3rd: Berry
4th: Floriana

Answers

120

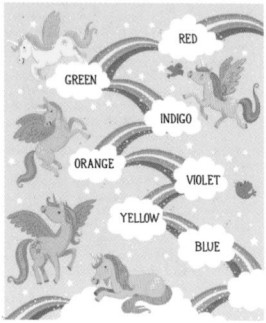

121 Hazel: 15
Daisy: 5
Moonbeam: 18
Alfie: 10

122

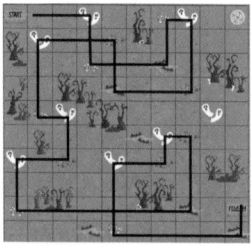

123

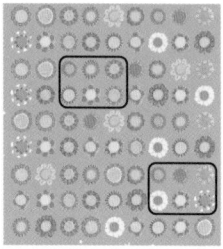

124

125 28 shoes

126

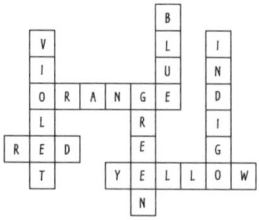

127

6	1	5	4	3	2
3	4	2	5	6	1
1	2	3	6	4	5
4	5	6	1	2	3
5	3	4	2	1	6
2	6	1	3	5	4

128 1st: Sunbeam
2nd: Dazzle
3rd: Thunder
4th: Sienna
5th: Leila

129

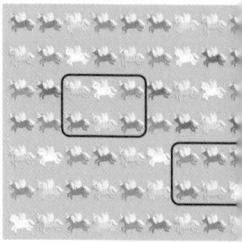

130

O	R	N	H
N	H	O	R
H	O	R	N
R	N	H	O